A BUG'S DAY

An Ant's Day

by Elizabeth Neuenfeldt

Illustrated by Claudia Marianno

BLASTOFF! MISSIONS

BLASTOFF! MISSIONS, AN IMPRINT OF BELLWETHER MEDIA BY FLUTTERBEE

Blastoff! Missions takes you on a learning adventure! Colorful illustrations and exciting narratives highlight cool facts about our world and beyond. Read the mission goals and follow the narrative to gain knowledge, build reading skills, and have fun!

Traditional Nonfiction

Narrative Nonfiction

Blastoff! Universe

MISSION GOALS

- FIND YOUR SIGHT WORDS IN THE BOOK.
- LEARN ABOUT THE DIFFERENT ROLES OF ANTS.
- LEARN ABOUT WHAT AN ANT DOES IN A DAY.

This edition first published in 2027 by Bellwether Media, Inc.

For information regarding permission, write to Bellwether Media, Inc., Attention: Permissions Department, 3500 American Blvd W, Suite 150, Bloomington, MN 55431.

Library of Congress Cataloging-in-Publication Data

Names: Neuenfeldt, Elizabeth author | Marianno, Claudia, illustrator. Title: An ant's day / by Elizabeth Neuenfeldt; illustrated by Claudia Marianno.
Description: Minneapolis, Minnesota : Bellwether Media, Inc., [2026] | Series: A bug's day | Includes bibliographical references and index. | Audience: Ages 5-8 | Audience: Grades 2-3 | Summary: "Vibrant illustrations accompany information about ants. The narrative nonfiction text is intended for students in kindergarten through third grade."-- Provided by publisher.
Identifiers: LCCN 2026001580 (print) | LCCN 2026001581 (ebook) | ISBN 9798898800901 (library binding) | ISBN 9798898802141 (ebook)
Subjects: LCSH: Ants--Behavior--Juvenile literature | Ants--Juvenile literature | Insects--Juvenile literature
Classification: LCC QL568.F7 N48 2026 (print) | LCC QL568.F7 (ebook)
LC record available at https://lccn.loc.gov/2026001580
LC ebook record available at https://lccn.loc.gov/2026001581

Editor: Betsy Rathburn Designer: Laura Sowers

Printed in the United States of America, North Mankato, MN.

This is **Blastoff Jimmy**! He is here to help you on your mission and share fun facts along the way!

Table of Contents

Working Hard

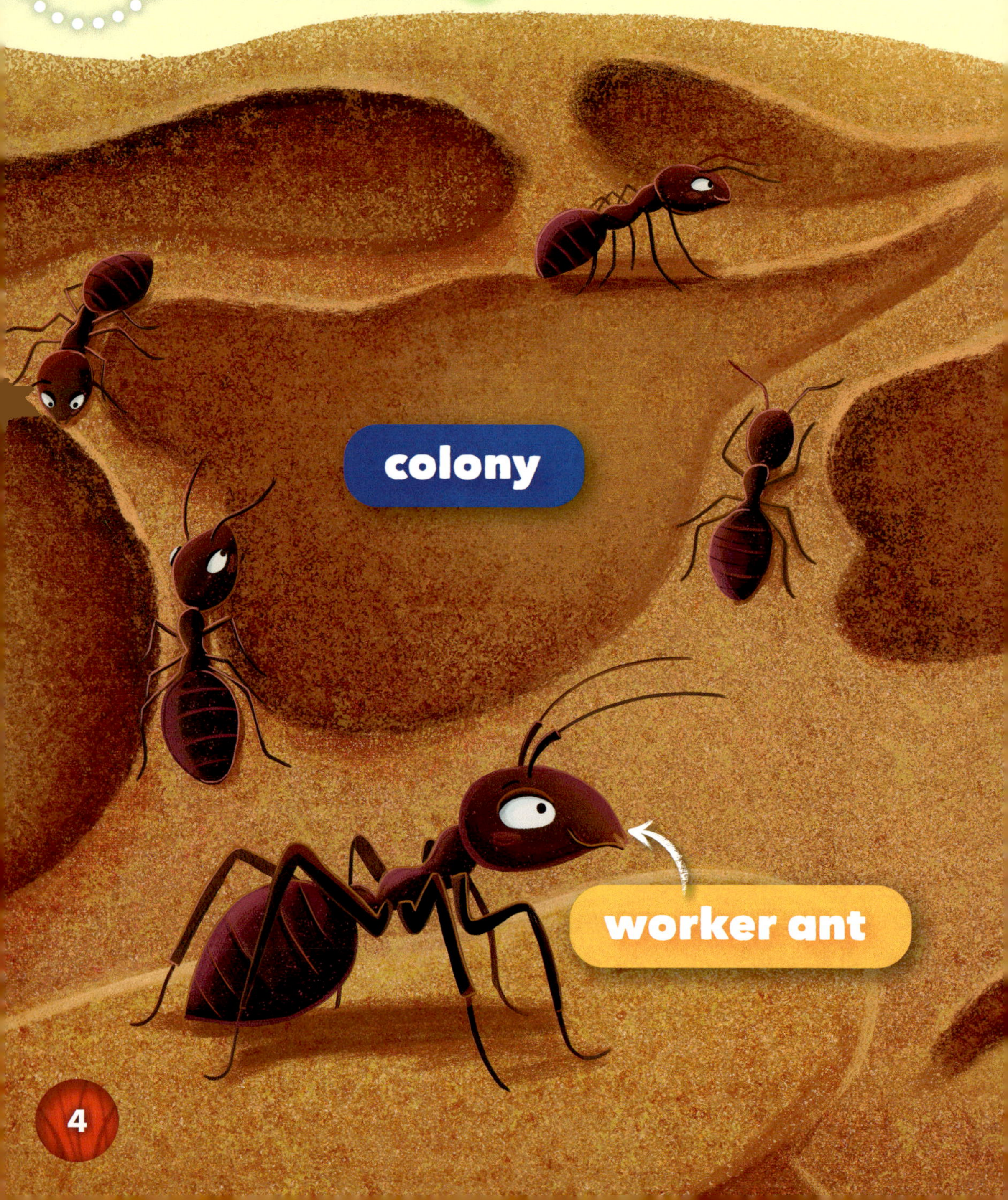

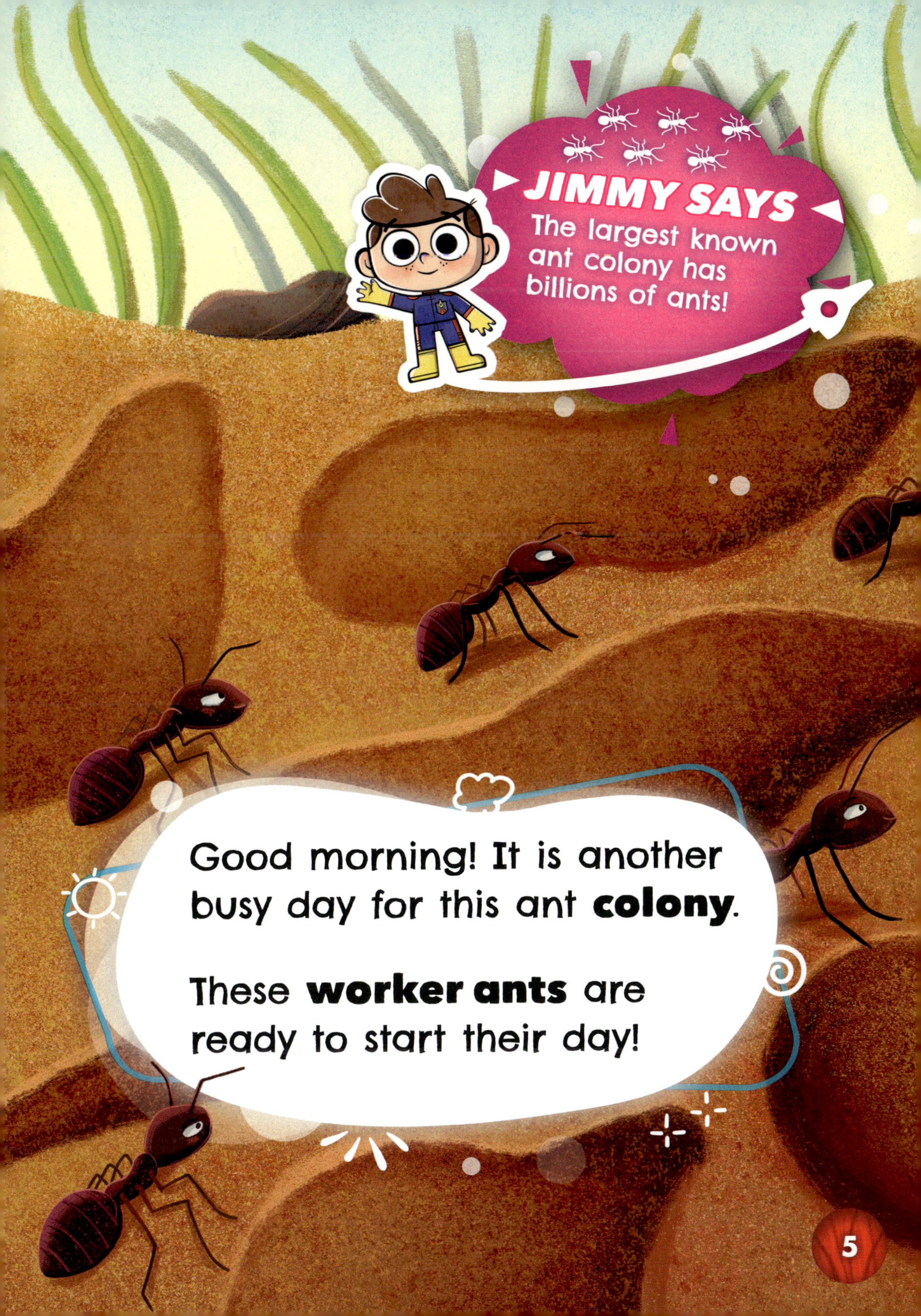

JIMMY SAYS
The largest known ant colony has billions of ants!

Good morning! It is another busy day for this ant **colony**.

These **worker ants** are ready to start their day!

Here comes the **queen**! She **mates** with **drones** and lays eggs.

Look at those young worker ants.
They care for eggs and **larvae**.

These worker ants are digging tunnels in the nest. They make the nest bigger.

Their work **aerates** the soil. It keeps the soil healthy!

JIMMY SAYS

The largest ant nest ever found was over 3,700 miles (5,955 kilometers) wide!

These older worker ants guard the nest. They watch out for birds, frogs, and other **predators**.

The workers seem worried.
Is danger near?

The guard workers' **pheromones** send out a warning. Danger is here. Everyone move! There is a beetle outside.

The workers **swarm**.
The enemy is defeated!

Finding Food

Now it is time to leave the nest. We will go look for food.

The worker ants walk through the tall grass. They find a bush with berries!

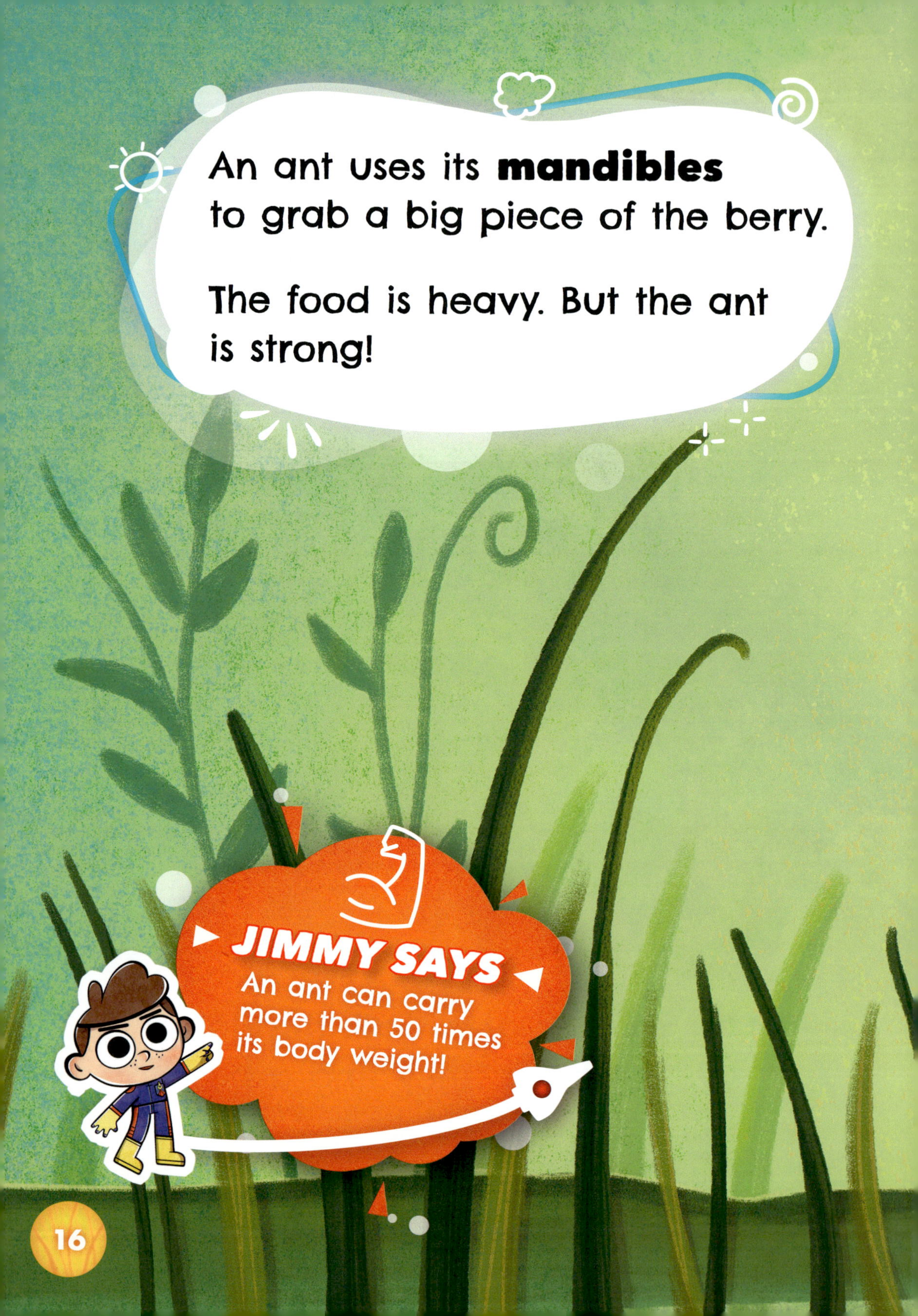

An ant uses its **mandibles** to grab a big piece of the berry.

The food is heavy. But the ant is strong!

JIMMY SAYS

An ant can carry more than 50 times its body weight!

mandibles

Back to the Colony

The worker ant leaves a trail of pheromones.

Other workers use their **antennae** to find the trail. They follow it to the sweet treat.

The worker ants bring food back to the colony. Dig in, everyone!

It has been a big day for these ants!

All About Ants

Body Parts

Things Seen

nest

tunnels

berries

Glossary

aerates–exposes to the air

antennae–feelers connected to an ant's head that sense information around them

colony–a group of ants

drones–male ants that mate with queen ants

larvae–young insects that break out of eggs and look like small worms

mandibles–jaws

mates–joins together to make young

pheromones–scents produced by ants that signal to other ants about food sources or danger

predators–animals that hunt other animals for food

queen–a female ant that lays eggs for its colony

swarm–to gather somewhere in large numbers

worker ants–female ants that gather food, care for the queen, and feed larvae

To Learn More

AT THE LIBRARY

Kenney, Karen Latchana. *All About Ants.* Minneapolis, Minn.: Jump!, 2024.

Leatherland, Noah. *Be an Ant Expert.* Minneapolis, Minn.: Bearport Publishing Company, 2025.

Pettiford, Rebecca. *Ants.* Minneapolis, Minn.: Bellwether Media, 2025.

ON THE WEB

FACTSURFER

Factsurfer.com gives you a safe, fun way to find more information.

1. Go to www.factsurfer.com.
2. Enter "an ant's day" into the search box and click 🔍.
3. Select your book cover to see a list of related content.

BEYOND THE MISSION

> WHAT FACT FROM THE BOOK DID YOU THINK WAS THE MOST INTERESTING?

> DRAW AN ANT. WHICH BODY PARTS DO YOU THINK ARE THE MOST USEFUL?

> ANTS DO MANY JOBS. WHICH JOB DO YOU THINK IS THE MOST IMPORTANT?

Index